DISGRACED!
The Dirty History of Performance-Enhancing Drugs in Sports™

THE NFL
Steroids and Human Growth Hormone

MICHAEL SOMMERS

rosen publishing's
rosen
central®

New York

11-24-09

To Oscar, Vladimir, and Tyrell for support and sustenance

Published in 2010 by The Rosen Publishing Group, Inc.
29 East 21st Street, New York, NY 10010

Library of Congress Cataloging-in-Publication Data

Sommers, Michael A., 1966–
The NFL: steroids and human growth hormone / Michael Sommers.—1st ed.
    p. cm.—(Disgraced! the dirty history of performance-enhancing drugs in sports)
Includes bibliographical references and index.
ISBN-13: 978-1-4358-5304-1 (library binding)
1. Football—Corrupt practices—United States—Juvenile literature. 2. Football players—Drug use—United States—Juvenile literature. 3. Doping in sports—United States—Juvenile literature. I. Title.
GV959.S58 2010
362.29—dc22

                                                            2008056131

Manufactured in the United States of America

CONTENTS

Introduction

Ever since humans first began playing games and sports, they have tried all sorts of ways of performing better than their rivals. Some achieved a competitive edge through hard work and training. Others relied on clever strategies. Then, there were those who turned to natural substances taken from plants and animals to boost their performances. Today, numerous substances known as performance-enhancing drugs (PEDs) are used by athletes to build strength, speed, and give them a competitive edge.

The most commonly used (and abused) PEDs are anabolic-androgenic steroids. "Anabolic" refers to muscle building. "Androgenic" refers to typical male characteristics like big muscles and a deep voice. Today's steroids are mostly manufactured substances whose effects are similar to those of testosterone, which is the primary male sex hormone. In some cases, steroids are helpful. Doctors prescribe them for certain medical problems or for men whose bodies don't make enough testosterone naturally. However, doctors are not supposed to prescribe them to athletes who are looking to build up their muscles and increase their size and strength. And using steroids without a prescription is illegal.

San Diego Chargers defensive lineman Shawne Merriman, seen here during a 2007 game against the Baltimore Ravens, tested positive for steroids in 2006.

Unfortunately, many players, coaches, doctors, and sports organizations have not played fair. Instead, they have acted as though the benefits of using steroids outweigh the dangers to athletes' health and the potential disgrace a player faces if the cheating is exposed. Nobody can deny that strength and speed are important for a professional ball player. However, when players' drug use comes to light, fans feel cheated and disappointed. Steroid scandals ruin the reputation of both the National Football League (NFL) and professional sports in America. They also ruin the good name, health, and sometimes even the lives of players who feel driven to use them. Instead of heroes, they end up losers.

Chapter 1

The Early Days

The long and complicated relationship between steroids and the NFL began in 1962. In July of that year, the San Francisco 49ers were at their training camp in the rolling hills of northern California. The setting was peaceful. However, for many players, the intense, twice-a-day practices were brutal.

The Case of Bob Waters

In an article published in the *New York Daily News* on June 16, 2008, writer Matt Chaney recalled the story of Bob Waters and the beginning of steroid use in the NFL. Waters, a third-year quarterback for the 49ers, was feeling bruised and beat up. He was tough and athletic, but he was also slim and compact. Despite measuring 6-foot-2 (1.89 meters), Waters weighed only 190 pounds (86 kilograms)—light as a feather in the NFL. Luckily, the team physician, Lloyd Millburn, had the perfect remedy for what ailed him: a brand-new wonder drug called Dianabol.

Seemingly overnight, Waters shot up to 210 pounds (5 kg). He continued to use "D-bol" for two years until his career ended, in 1965, as a result of injuries. At the time, a five-year career in the NFL was normal. After retiring, Waters became a college football coach at Western Carolina. He never blamed steroids for the terrible disease he developed in the 1980s: amyotrophic lateral sclerosis (ALS). Also known as Lou Gehrig's disease, ALS is a fatal disease that attacks the

"D-bol"

Dianabol is the trade name for the anabolic steroid methandrostenolone, which comes in pill form. It was introduced in the United States in 1958. Originally, doctors used it to treat medical conditions. When physician Lloyd Millburn prescribed it to quarterback Bob Waters to help him get bigger and stronger, Waters became the earliest confirmed anabolic-steroid user in the history of professional football in the United States.

In 2008, Dianabol turned fifty years old. The brand-name drug is no longer manufactured in the United States. However, generic methandrostenolone continues to be used by athletes all over the world.

One of the biggest names in pro football in the 1960s, quarterback Bob Waters played for the San Francisco 49ers from 1960 to 1965.

nerve cells in the brain. It results in gradual paralysis of all muscles, including those that control speech, swallowing, and even breathing. There is no certain link between steroid use and ALS. Waters died in 1989. He was only fifty years old.

Alvin Roy: Steroid Guru

Chaney's *New York Daily News* article also told how strength coach Alvin Roy recommended steroids to players early on. Roy brought the drugs along with him when he started his new job with the San Diego Chargers in July 1963. At the Chargers camp in Southern California, Roy and head coach Sid Gillman began giving Dianabol to players. The Chargers were told that the pink pills contained protein.

"If Alvin had said 'steroids,' we [the players] wouldn't have known anyway," recalled Ron Mix, a Hall of Fame lineman who was the Chargers'

Sid Gillman, seen here in San Diego in 1971, coached the Chargers from 1960 to 1971.

captain. Chaney quoted Mix as saying, "They had the pills set out in cereal bowls. We were told to take a pill after every meal, and we did. And they actually worked. Normally in training camp, I'd feel my strength going down, but it actually increased."

Mix told Chaney that, soon after the entire team began taking daily steroids, a player mentioned Roy's method to his family doctor. The doctor was concerned about potential side effects. When confronted by Mix, Gillman assured players that the drugs were safe. Mix, however, told his buddies about the risks, which ranged from hair loss and severe pimples to irrational, violent behavior (later termed "'roid rage"), liver disease, and heart problems. According to Mix, both he and most of his teammates stopped taking the "protein pills."

A Dirty Secret

During the 1960s, few people in the sports world talked about the use of steroids. However, within pro football circles, the use of D-bol and other, newer anabolic steroids continued to increase. Then, in the 1970s, steroid use really took off. Weightlifting had become a popular training activity, and suddenly, every football player had to have a buffed, bulked-up body. Most could get big by lifting weights and drinking protein shakes. But those looking for a shortcut could achieve results faster by taking steroids, too.

Nicknamed "'roids" or "juice," steroids were already popular on the professional weightlifting circuit, so football players who worked out in weightlifting gyms were exposed to steroids. The drugs became widely acceptable in sports circles—and easy to get.

The World of PEDs

Anabolic steroids can be obtained legally with a doctor's prescription, but many are purchased illegally through dealers in gyms, locker rooms, magazines, or over the Internet. Aside from anabolic steroids, other types of popular PEDs have been banned by the NFL. These include:

- **Ephedrine** is an ingredient made from a Chinese herb, ephedra, which is used in diet pills, energy boosters, and sports supplements. The effects of ephedrine are similar to those of the drug known as speed (amphetamines). Taking ephedrine can help athletes develop lean muscle mass, and it makes them hyper-alert and quick to react. Side effects include heart attacks and strokes. To date, ephedrine has been linked to more than one hundred deaths in the United States. In 2004, ephedrine was banned by the U.S. government.
- **Tetrahydrogestrinone (THG)** is known as a "designer" steroid because it was designed to be undetectable by drug tests. It comes

in transparent liquid form, leading to its popular nickname, "the Clear." THG hasn't been approved for use by the U.S. government. Selling or using it is illegal.

- **Androstenedione (andro)** became very popular after baseball slugger Mark McGwire admitted to using it in 1998. (Major League Baseball had not banned the substance yet.) Athletes use andro because it raises testosterone levels to far above normal. Side effects are the same as those of anabolic steroids. However, andro is harder to detect in urine tests. The U.S. government banned the sale of andro and other steroid-like dietary supplements in 2005.

The Chargers' Ron Mix faces down the opposition in 1967. When he discovered he was being given steroids, he stopped taking them.

- **Furosemide** is a drug that is used by people who want to lose weight quickly. It is a diuretic, which means that it works to flush out other substances in the body, via urination. Athletes often use furosemide before getting tested in an attempt to mask the presence of other drugs in their systems. Like all diuretics, furosemide can be dangerous if taken in high doses.

- **Erythropoietien (EPO)** is a hormone, or a compound that is released by the body's glands to regulate body functions. EPO is naturally produced by the kidneys. When extra EPO is injected into an athlete's bloodstream (a process known as blood doping), the blood is able to carry more oxygen than usual to muscles in the body. This allows athletes to work longer and harder. EPO is especially popular with endurance athletes, such as long-distance runners and cyclists. On the downside, EPO is linked to clogged arteries and heart failure.

- **Human growth hormone (HGH)** is a substance that is produced by the pituitary gland. It increases muscle mass and lowers body fat. If a patient doesn't have sufficient natural levels of HGH, doctors sometimes prescribe injections of manufactured HGH. As a performance-enhancing drug, HGH is used by athletes who believe it will help them produce sudden bursts of strength. Such athletes include sprinters, weightlifters, and football players. Taking HGH can decrease the chance of injury. The side effects, however, can be serious. They range from increased blood pressure, fluid retention, and swollen and deformed joints to the development of such life-threatening conditions as diabetes, irregular heart rhythms, and failure of the pituitary gland.

Chapter 2

PEDs Go Public

By the mid-1980s, so many NFL players were using steroids that the problem could no longer be ignored. Many were worried about what the drugs were doing to athletes' bodies. But more and more, the mounting pressure to win was only possible with the help of PEDs.

Testing

In 1986, the NFL began testing players for drug use. In 1986, 30 percent of all players tested positive for steroids, meaning that they had traces of steroids in their urine. However, Dr. Forest Tennant, drug adviser to the NFL, estimated that perhaps 50 percent of all linemen and linebackers—positions requiring especially big and bulky players—were using steroids at the time. After stepping down from his job, Tennant admitted in a 1991 interview with the *New York Times* that the NFL had ignored steroid abuse for years.

At first, players who were discovered with steroids in their systems received only a warning as punishment. In 1989, when the NFL began to suspend players for steroid use, a first offense resulted in a suspension of no more than thirty days. In 1990, the league began a policy of random testing that took place during both the regular season and the off-season. But in his 1991 interview with the *New York Times*, Tennant indicated that this policy may not be completely effective, saying that "random testing [for steroids] only tests a handful of people, and it doesn't get to the guys who are known to have used them."

Steak, Potatoes, and Milkshakes

Pro football Hall of Famer Eugene "Gene" Upshaw played guard for the Oakland Raiders for fifteen seasons. He later served as executive director of the NFL Players Association (NFLPA) from 1983 until his death in 2008. Upshaw blamed the NFL for its players' problems with steroids.

"Teams draft a kid who looks like he can be a player," Upshaw told the *New York Times* in 1991. "But when they get the player at mini camp, they see that he's smaller and not as strong as they thought. They tell him that he's got to be bigger and stronger before he reports to training camp, and he's got eight weeks to do it. There's only so many steak, potatoes, and milkshakes you can eat in eight weeks. If the player is up against a time frame, he'll do what he has to do to get the results."

Lyle Alzado

Lyle Alzado of the Oakland Raiders was as famous for his tough defense as he was for his colorful personality and crazy (often violent) antics. During his long career, which lasted throughout the 1970s and 1980s, Alzado played for the Raiders, the Cleveland Browns, and the Denver Broncos. In his career, he made almost 1,000 tackles, recorded 97 sacks, and forced 24 fumbles. He played in two Super Bowls, claiming victory in one. However, all of his accomplishments on the field are overshadowed by the fact that he was the

Football legend Lyle Alzado was famous for his on-field ferocity. He is seen here in 1984 during Super Bowl XVIII in Tampa, Florida. After his retirement, Alzado admitted to being a former steroid user.

Legendary lineman Lyle Alzado looks on as his former team, the Los Angeles Raiders, wins a victory over the Denver Broncos in 1991.

first major U.S. pro athlete to admit to using steroids. For many fans, the disgrace of his admission cancels out all of his achievements.

Alzado's use of steroids and HGH came to light as he was battling a brain tumor at the age of forty-two. Although some doctors disagreed, Alzado believed that his long-term use of steroids was responsible for his illness. In a moving 1991 interview with *Sports Illustrated*, he spoke about being sick:

"Everyone knows me as a tough, tough guy. And I've never been afraid of anything. Not any human, not anything. Then I woke up in the hospital last March and they told me, 'You have cancer.' Cancer. I couldn't understand it. All I knew was that I was just so weak. I went through all those wars on the football field. I was so muscular. I was a giant. Now I'm sick. And I'm scared."

The brain tumor that caused Lyle Alzado's symptoms eventually took his life in May 1992.

Chapter 3

Team Steroid

Lyle Alzado was the first NFL football player to come forward and publicly warn of the destructive effects that steroids have on an individual player. Steve Courson, an offensive lineman with the Pittsburgh Steelers, went even further. Courson blew the whistle on his entire team.

Courson was inspired by Alzado's gutsy confession and was ashamed of his own history of steroid use. In 1991, the man nicknamed "Mr. Steeler" published his autobiography, *False Glory: Steelers and Steroids: The Steve Courson Story*. In his book, Courson wrote about how he used steroids throughout his entire career. He began "juicing up" occasionally when playing college ball at the University of South Carolina. However, by the time he was playing pro ball with the Steelers (1978–1983), the massive linebacker had come to rely upon regular injections of steroids. In his last two years as a pro with the Tampa Bay Buccaneers, Courson needed the steroids to keep from feeling the effects of injuries and age.

The Steelers of the 1970s

The Pittsburgh Steelers are one of the oldest and most successful teams in American pro football. Between 1974 and 1979, they made history by winning four Super Bowl titles. However, during this time, America's top team was fueled by drugs, according to Courson. In *False Glory*, Courson claims that team owner Art Rooney and head coach Chuck Noll tolerated the use of "juice" to make players bigger, stronger, and faster.

From 1978 to 1983, Steve Courson was an offensive lineman for the Pittsburgh Steelers. Above, he is seen in a 1981 game at Three Rivers Stadium. Courson shocked football fans when he admitted he'd used steroids during his time in Pittsburgh.

In the 1960s and 1970s, steroids like D-bol were manufactured legally by Ciba Pharmaceuticals, a company based in New Jersey. It was easy to get a doctor's prescription for these seemingly harmless pills, but they could also be easily acquired at weightlifting gyms.

Courson's confessions shocked America. The NFL and Steelers officials strongly denied any knowledge of steroid use, but people did question the Steelers' winning streak. How much had been due to real talent, and how much was because of drugs? In a 2005 interview published in the *Pittsburgh Tribune*, Courson declared that the Steelers would have won their Super Bowls even without steroids, "as long as everyone else wasn't on the juice."

In April 2005, former Pittsburgh Steelers star Steve Courson testified before the U.S. House of Representatives about the use of PEDs in professional football.

When Courson's book hit the shelves, many in the NFL, including his old teammates, turned their backs on him. However, the public and even the U.S. government sat up and took notice. In 2005, Courson was invited to Washington, D.C., to testify before Congress, which, concerned with steroid scandals, had begun investigations into the use of PEDs in professional sports. Congress praised Courson for his knowledge and his courage to speak out.

Following his retirement from pro football, Courson traveled the country, talking to students about the dangers of steroid use. He knew about the dangers firsthand. Courson blamed his steroid use for the weakening of his heart, a condition that threatened his life as he waited four years for an organ transplant.

The York Connection

Based in York, Pennsylvania, York Barbell is the oldest manufacturer of weightlifting and fitness equipment in the United States. At the company's factory gyms in the 1960s and 1970s, steroids were seen as just another way to increase strength, like barbells and weight belts. In his June 2008 *New York Daily News* article about Dianabol, Matt Chaney reported that strength coach Alvin Roy was part of the so-called "York Gang" that distributed steroids to football players. Roy not only had his own gym in Baton Rouge, Louisiana, but he also went on to work as a coach for the Kansas City Chiefs, Dallas Cowboys, and Oakland Raiders after his first job with the San Diego Chargers.

Another member of the York Gang was the "Godfather of Steroids," Dr. John Ziegler. According to Chaney, he was responsible for bringing steroids to America from Russia. Ziegler, a big and tough former Marine, was both a medical doctor and a chemist who worked at Ciba. In his spare time, he loved to pump iron. And it was he who served as the steroid link between Ciba and its now-famous gym in York, Pennsylvania. At the York gym, he began distributing the steroids in small doses to weightlifters and other athletes, all of whom wanted "Doc Ziegler's mysterious pink pills."

At the time, most football players didn't even know what steroids were, and they weren't aware of the long-term risks involved. The drugs were just viewed as a training supplement that could be used to get a competitive edge. The only problem was that, in order to get even more of an edge, some started taking far more pills than Ziegler and other specialists recommended.

Courson overcame his heart problems without a transplant. But in 2005, he died in a freak accident while cutting down a tree on his Pennsylvania property. On his computer, friends found a letter in which he expressed his disappointment that more players weren't honest about their steroid use.

Steroid Curse

Courson's early death wasn't due to steroids, but his weak heart was. Courson was only one of an astonishing eighteen former Steelers from the 1970s and 1980s who died young and had horrible deaths in the years since

Fans pack Pittsburgh's Three Rivers Stadium in 1975. The Steelers were the most dominant team in the NFL during the 1970s and early 1980s, winning the Super Bowl in 1975, 1976, 1979, and 1980.

2000. Apart from the fact that they all played for Pittsburgh, there has been some speculation that some of those players may have used steroids or other illegal performance-enhancing drugs. The most common cause of death was heart failure, which affected seven players: Jim Clack, fifty-eight years old; Ray Oldham, fifty-four; Dave Brown, fifty-two; Mike Webster, fifty; Steve Furness, forty-nine; Joe Gilliam, forty-nine; and Tyrone McGriff, forty-one.

The string of deaths shocked more than just football fans and the city of Pittsburgh. It really brought attention to the dangers of steroids in professional football, even after a user's playing days are through.

Chapter 4

Super Scandals

Beginning in 2000, athletes' use of steroids, HGH, and other supplements was occurring on a major scale. Steroid scandals were exploding as never before, involving highly organized groups that included lab specialists, sellers, dealers, and athletes. The amounts of money involved were enormous. So, too, was the monetary payoff for the pro athletes and teams that found a way to win.

BALCO Scandal

One of the biggest steroid scandals in pro sports was known as "the BALCO affair." BALCO (Bay Area Laboratory Co-Operative) was a California-based company owned by Victor Conte. BALCO began as a lab that analyzed blood and urine for drug tests. It also sold food supplements to athletes. However, an investigation in 2003 found that Conte was also selling "the Clear" and HGH to athletes, many of whom were big-name international sports stars.

When the truth came out, the world was shocked to discover that BALCO clients included Olympic champion sprinter Marion Jones, cyclist Tammy Thomas, and, most famously, baseball star Barry Bonds. Others discovered to be BALCO customers were various players from the Oakland Raiders, including Barret Robbins, Chris Cooper, Dana Stubblefield, and Bill Romanowski. All of these players tested positive for "the Clear" in 2003.

The founder of BALCO, Victor Conte, is shown here with the media in September 2005. Conte was sentenced in federal court for his role in supplying athletes with steroids.

Dana Stubblefield

Dana Stubblefield, a defensive lineman, was the first football player to be prosecuted. In a courtroom, he admitted to lying to federal agents about his use of EPO and "the Clear," both of which he had received from BALCO in 2003. NFL drug tests proved that Stubblefield had lied days after he had denied using the steroids. The NFL suspended him for four games. However, by the end of the season, the former All-Pro had retired in a cloud of shame over his steroid use.

Called to testify before a grand jury in 2007, Stubblefield admitted that Conte had supplied him with "the Clear." He said Conte told him it was an unidentifiable, steroid-like substance that would help him recover from injuries. Stubblefield also confessed that he let Conte inject him with EPO. He claimed that Conte promised him the NFL didn't test for EPO but at the same time warned him to keep quiet about the injections he was receiving.

Bill Romanowski

Another high-profile user whose career was troubled by his involvement in the BALCO affair was Bill Romanowski. "Romo," as he was known, had a reputation as one of the NFL's best linebackers. In a career spanning sixteen years, Romanowski played for four teams and won four Super Bowls. However, he was also known to be especially mean and violent on the field. He racked up many fines for brutal behavior that included breaking fingers, busting jaws, and even crushing one opponent's eye socket.

In a 2005 interview with CBS News, Romanowski was asked what drove him to act as if he were in a permanent state of 'roid rage. "A fear of failure," he answered. "The fear of not being good enough . . . In professional football, the competition is so intense. 'Is he good enough? Is he fast enough? Does he hit people hard enough? Does he get hurt a lot?' . . . I didn't want to lose my job."

Romanowski said this pressure pushed him over the edge in terms of his aggressive behavior. It also led him to gain an edge by any means possible. Over the years, Romanowski became obsessed with supplements. He admits that he spent more than $200,000 a year on drugs, doctors, and therapists. He took more than one hundred pills a day and tried all sorts of alternative therapies to make him tougher and stronger. For a time, he injected himself with cells from Scottish black sheep to help heal injuries. Often, he didn't even know what doctors were giving him. But in his book, *Romo: My Life on the Edge*, he did admit to taking steroids between 2001 and 2003.

Romanowski recalls that BALCO's Conte gave him capsules full of bitter-tasting yellow fluid that he referred to as "pro-hormones." He claims it was only later that he discovered it was a new anabolic steroid known as THG. In his book, Romo also admitted to taking "the Cream" and HGH. But as soon as he found out that they were something he could be tested for, he stopped taking them. As he stated in the CBS interview, he was prepared to cheat in order

Denver Bronco powerhouse Bill Romanowski tackles an opposing player in the opening game of the 2000 season.

"to get ahead, to play another year, to play two more years, to win another Super Bowl."

Romanowski had the kind of football career that might eventually land a player in the Hall of Fame. However, in light of his involvement in one of the biggest steroid scandals in history, it seems unlikely that Romo will be heading to Canton anytime soon.

Super Bowl Scandal

In early 2005, sports fans across America were surprised to find out that three players from the Carolina Panthers had bought and used illegal PEDs in the weeks leading up to the 2004 Super Bowl. The Patriots won the game, but in the end, the Panthers received most of the attention—for all the wrong reasons.

On March 30, 2005, the CBS news television program *60 Minutes* reported that in 2005, federal investigators were looking into the case of a South Carolina physician named Dr. James Shortt. Shortt had been accused of killing a patient after giving her an alternative drug treatment. While going through Shortt's records, investigators uncovered evidence showing that Shortt had written prescriptions for Panthers players, allowing them to obtain steroids and other PEDs. The discovery set off a scandal involving center Jeff Mitchell, tackle Todd Steussie, and punter Todd Sauerbraun. Only ten days prior to the Super Bowl game, all three players filled prescriptions for a steroid banned by the NFL.

Carolina Panthers center Jeff Mitchell faces down the Tampa Bay Buccaneers in 2005. That year, news broke that Mitchell and other Panthers had attempted to acquire steroids before the Super Bowl.

According to the *60 Minutes* program, further investigations found that Steussie and Mitchell had been using testosterone ointment over an eight-year period. Known as "the Cream," the main ingredient of this substance is the male hormone testosterone. Aside from "the Cream," Sauerbraun also purchased syringes (needles) and the steroid Stanozolol. Stanozolol made headlines when Canadian sprinter Ben Johnson used it during the 1988 Olympic Games. The discovery that steroids were responsible for his gold medal victory shocked the world. Publicly disgraced, Johnson was stripped of his medal, and his sprinting career never recovered. (It is interesting to note, however, that the day after the

A Shameful End

PEDs could not help Bill Romanowski absorb all of the serious hits that he took over the years, including the nearly twenty concussions he suffered. By 2003, he had trouble with his balance, his sight, and even processing words and thoughts. By the time the BALCO scandal hit, Romanowski had already been forced to retire from the game.

According to Romanowski, the most shameful part about his steroid use was the embarrassment he felt in front of the NFL, his teammates, his friends, and especially his family. Then, his son found out about his drug use from the kids at school. "That one hurt me more than anything," Romanowski confessed to CBS.

scandal broke, recruiters for two NFL teams contacted him about the possibility of playing for their teams.)

News of the Panthers' drug use was equally shocking. Sports fans were outraged that such brazen cheating had tainted one of America's most popular and cherished sporting events. The scandal raised serious questions about the NFL's drug-testing program.

Testing Flaws

Until the Super Bowl scandal broke, the NFL had a reputation for having one of the strictest antidrug policies in U.S. pro sports. But if that was the case, how was it that testing failed to catch the three Panthers' use of banned and illegal drugs? The problem was that even as testing standards had become tougher,

Chicago's Todd Sauerbraun punts during a 1995 game. At one time, Sauerbraun was considered to be the top-rated punter in the NFL.

those who prescribe and use steroids have become sneakier. Increasingly, they use drugs that don't show up in regular tests.

Testing for testosterone, a hormone that naturally appears at various levels in all males, is very difficult. According to the international antidrug standards followed by the NFL, use of PEDs can be confirmed only if an athlete's testosterone levels are four times higher than normal. "The Cream" used by the Panthers leaves just very small traces in urine, especially when taken along with "the Clear."

Sauerbraun's use of Stanozolol was more complicated. Dr. Charles E. Yesalis II, a professor at Penn State University, is one of the nation's leading experts on PEDs. Asked to comment on the scandal, Yesalis pointed out in an interview published in the *Chicago Tribune*, "Nobody in his right mind would have taken [Stanozolol], unless they weren't worried about being tested."

The NFL responded to the scandal by noting that every week it carries out random testing on players from all NFL teams. Moreover, during a 2004 inquiry by Congress into the problem of PEDs in pro sports, NFL commissioner Paul Tagliabue claimed that the league spent more than $10 million a year on drug testing.

David Black, a forensic toxicologist (specialist in drugs), helped develop the NFL's drug-testing program back in the late 1980s. In an interview broadcast on the *60 Minutes* news program, he admitted to being very skeptical that use of such drugs could have escaped detection. According to records obtained by *60 Minutes*, Sauerbraun, the NFL's top-rated punter, was at one point receiving shockingly large injections of Stanozolol. As Black told the *60 Minutes* interviewer, "In my wildest expectations, I could not imagine someone using [so much] Stanozolol, competing in the NFL." He added that the steroid not only increases muscle mass but gives athletes an unfair advantage by making them more aggressive and mentally alert. He recalled that when he took the drug himself as part of a lab experiment, he felt as if he were eighteen again instead of forty.

Chapter 5

Steroid Nation

Between 2005 and the day in April 2007 when federal agents raided his house, former bodybuilder David Jacobs manufactured illegal steroids in his suburban Texas home. Jacobs had set up his own lab. Using measuring cups and pots on the stove, he mixed and heated chemical powders into powerful steroids that he sold to dealers across the United States. Jacobs also smuggled synthetic HGH into the United States from China. He sold it as well.

Operation Raw Deal

In November 2008, Jacobs pleaded guilty to charges of distributing illegal steroids. In April 2005, he was sentenced to three years of probation. The crackdown on Jacobs was part of Operation Raw Deal, a federal investigation targeting those who imported and sold illegal PEDs.

On May 2, 2008, the *New York Times* ran an article by Michael S. Schmidt. In it, Schmidt reported that Jacobs confessed that two of the dealers with whom he worked were NFL players. Jacobs identified one of the players as Matt Lehr, a lineman for the New Orleans Saints. Although Lehr's lawyer denied that the player ever sold PEDs, Lehr tested positive for using a banned substance in 2006. As punishment, he was suspended for four games.

Equally disturbing was Jacobs's claim that he regularly gave advice to NFL players on how to take advantage of weaknesses in the NFL's drug-testing program. On the Web site for his supplements store, Jacobs wrote that he had

Matt Lehr of the New Orleans Saints, seen here during a 2008 game against the Kansas City Chiefs, received a four-game suspension in 2006.

counseled players from the Atlanta Falcons and the Dallas Cowboys. An example of advice that Jacobs gave players was telling them to use steroids only in the off-season because only four thousand of the twelve thousand yearly tests that the NFL performs on its players take place in the off-season. Consequently, players use HGH (which can't be detected by testing) throughout the year. And to reduce their chances of getting caught, they use steroids only when they aren't playing. They also use masking drugs.

After receiving his sentence, Jacobs agreed to cooperate with NFL officials who wanted to find out about the players involved in the case. According to Schmidt's *New York Times* article, Jacobs stated that he would tell the NFL about the problems with its drug program but would reveal the players' identities only if the NFL promised "their lives won't be destroyed like mine." Later that same month, Jacobs provided names to NFL officials who promised to investigate and punish any players found to have used drugs.

Tragically, Jacobs and his girlfriend were found shot to death in his home in June 2008. The police called the deaths a murder-suicide. Before his death, Jacobs gave an interview in which he declared that pro football is full of drug users. Meanwhile, the NFL has yet to dole out punishments to any players who might have been dealers or users of drugs sold by Jacobs.

Looking Into the Future

"The use of performance-enhancing drugs like steroids in baseball, football, and other sports is dangerous and sends the wrong message: that there are shortcuts to accomplishment, and that performance is more important than character." —President George W. Bush, State of the Union Address, January 20, 2004

In the last few years, the use of PEDs in professional sports has gone from being a dirty little secret to a major issue debated at the highest levels of government. In response to the drug scandals of the last few years, Congress has held investigations on how to clean up pro sports. Among the professional leagues that came under fire was the NFL. However, according to a 2008 article on ESPN.com, the NFL has one of the best antidrug programs of any of the pro

In March 2004, NFL commissioner Paul Tagliabue *(left)* testifies about drug testing policies in pro football before a U.S. Senate committee in Washington, D.C.

sports leagues in America. It was the first league to begin doing serious drug testing, and all players are tested at least once during the regular season. On the downside, this universal testing is carried out at training camps. The fact that players know in advance when they will be tested allows them to prepare for tests by temporarily stopping steroid use or using drugs that mask the presence of banned substances.

Other forms of testing are tougher, even though they don't affect all players. Every week, for example, even during the off-season, ten athletes from each team are chosen to undergo random testing without warning. And the NFL has

Masking Drugs

According to *New York Times* reporter Michael S. Schmidt, steroid dealer David Jacobs had many solutions for players who didn't want to get caught using drugs. He sold an herbal supplement that flushed steroids out of their bodies quickly. This way, even if the players were using banned drugs, traces wouldn't be detected in urine tests. Jacobs also suggested that players get team doctors to write them prescriptions for drugs that would hide their steroid use. One of the most popular of these masking drugs, finasteride, is used to treat balding in young men. To get it, players go to their doctors and complain that their hair is thinning due to the constant rubbing of their helmets against their scalps. As of the end of 2008, the NFL still had not added finasteride to its list of banned substances.

Convicted steroid dealer David Jacobs is seen here at home on April 30, 2008, shortly before his death.

also begun doing random CIR testing. "CIR" stands for carbon isotope ratio. CIR testing involves a more thorough examination of urine samples, which can show whether or not an athlete is using testosterone creams.

Light Punishment

Perhaps the biggest problem is what happens to players who test positive for PEDs: not much. Players who test positive have their names released, but the drugs they use are not revealed. Moreover, the punishments these players receive are not severe. The first time a player is caught, he is suspended from playing four games. The second time, he is suspended for eight games.

Patriots' safety Rodney Harrison is one example. In an article published by the ESPN.com news service on September 2, 2007, reporter Chris Mortensen wrote that Harrison admitted to federal investigators that he had obtained and used HGH. Harrison served a four-game suspension but maintained that he used the banned substance to help him heal from an injury and not to gain a competitive edge. His explanation wasn't very convincing, as investigators discovered that Harrison had received a package of HGH with his name on it before he played in the 2004 Super Bowl game that brought scandal upon the Carolina Panthers. Confessions and evidence aside, Harrison continues to play with the Patriots.

Shawne Merriman is another player who tested positive for steroid use and received a four-game suspension. According to an October 24, 2008, article published in the *New York Times*, in 2006, the San Diego Chargers linebacker was found with traces of the steroid nandrolone in his system. Merriman said the positive test was the result of using a legal, over-the-counter diet supplement that was tainted. On one hand, the episode led to the creation of the so-called Merriman Rule. This rule bans all players who tested positive for steroids from playing in the Pro Bowl or winning any awards for their performance during that same season. However, before the rule could go into effect, Merriman did play in the Pro Bowl. In an interview published in the *Denver Post*, he claimed that he was "not embarrassed" despite the scandal. As of the end of 2008, Merriman is still playing in the NFL.

Above, safety Rodney Harrison of the New England Patriots has just completed a successful tackle in 2007 game against the Dallas Cowboys. Harrison received a four-day suspension in 2007 for using HGH.

In the End . . .

If PED users don't have to worry about their reputations or their careers, they do have to be concerned about their health and the rest of their lives. The long-term use of steroids has a major impact on the functioning of the brain. It can lead to mood swings, aggressiveness, and violent behavior. It also leads to serious and permanent physical problems. For men, steroids mess with masculine traits, causing testicles to shrink, infertility, baldness, and the development of breasts. Severe acne and trembling are also common. Dangers of long-term steroid use include fluid retention, high cholesterol and blood pressure, kidney failure, liver damage, and heart disease. Taking PEDs may allow players to win a game or even enjoy a Super Bowl–winning season. Over the long run, however, PED users lose big time—often cutting short their careers and destroying their lives, which is a real disgrace.

anabolic Muscle building.

anabolic steroids Testosterone-based drugs that are used by some athletes to increase weight and strength by increasing muscle mass.

brazen Bold and full of contempt.

"the Clear" Slang term for THG, a clear substance (whose ingredients include steroids) that is a dietary supplement and also a popular PED, since it's hard to detect during drug tests.

"the Cream" Slang term for a performance-enhancing drug in ointment form whose main ingredient is testosterone.

Dianabol Also known as D-bol, an anabolic steroid in pill form that was first used in the United States in the late 1950s.

diuretic Substance that increases the volume of urine being expelled from the body.

hormones Compounds formed in the glands that circulate throughout the body to regulate functions. Scientists also make artificial hormones for medical use.

human growth hormone (HGH) Hormone that increases muscle mass and lowers body fat. It is naturally produced by the pituitary gland but can be manufactured as well.

juice Slang expression for steroids.

performance-enhancing drug (PED) Term given to any type of substance used by athletes (often illegally) to improve their performance.

'roid rage Expression used to describe the uncontrolled and violent behavior displayed by people who abuse steroids.

supplement Vitamin, mineral, or other substance taken in addition to what the body normally requires.

synthetic Manufactured, rather than produced naturally.

syringe Hypodermic needle used for injections.

testosterone Hormone that appears naturally in all males and is responsible for typical masculine characteristics.

FOR MORE INFORMATION

Association Against Steroid Abuse
521 N. Sam Houston Parkway E., Suite 635
Houston, TX 77060
Web site: http://www.steroidabuse.com
This educational organization fights against the abuse of anabolic steroids.

Canadian Centre for Ethics in Sport (CCES)
350–955 Green Valley Crescent
Ottawa, ON K2C 3V4
Canada
(613) 521-3340
Web site: http://www.cces.ca
The CCES is involved in research and education relevant to fair play and drug-free
    sports. It also administers Canada's antidrug program.

National Center for Drug Free Sport, Inc.
2537 Madison Avenue
Kansas City, MO 64108
(816) 474-8655
Web site: http://www.drugfreesport.com
Drug Free Sport offers innovative alternatives to traditional drug-use prevention
    programs for athletic organizations across the country.

National Football League (NFL)
280 Park Avenue, 15th Floor
New York, NY 10017
(212) 450-2000
Web site: http://www.nfl.com
The NFL governs play in America's largest professional football league.

National Institute on Drug Abuse (NIDA)
6001 Executive Boulevard
Bethesda, MD 20892-9561
(301) 443-1124
Web site: http://www.nida.nih.gov
A branch of the National Institutes of Health, NIDA is the world's largest supporter
   of research focusing on drug abuse. It also works to improve the prevention
   and treatment of drug addiction.

World Anti-Doping Agency (WADA)
Stock Exchange Tower
800 Place Victoria, Suite 1700
P.O. Box 120
Montreal, QC H4Z 1B7
Canada
(514) 904-9232
Web site: http://www.wada-ama.org/en
WADA's mission is to monitor and fight against the use of all forms of PEDs in
   all international sports.

Web Sites

Due to the changing nature of Internet links, Rosen Publishing has developed
an online list of Web sites related to the subject of this book. This site is
updated regularly. Please use this link to access the list:

http://www.rosenlinks.com/dis/foot

FOR FURTHER READING

Aretha, David. *Steroids and Other Performance-Enhancing Drugs*. Berkeley Heights, NJ: MyReportLinks.com Books, 2005.

Courson, Steve. *False Glory: Steelers and Steroids: The Steve Courson Story*. Stamford, CT: Longmeadow Press, 1991.

Deuker, Carl. *Gym Candy*. Boston, MA: Graphia, 2008.

Lau, Doretta. *Steroids* (Incredibly Disgusting Drugs). New York, NY: Rosen Publishing, 2008.

Monroe, Judy. *Steroids, Sports, and Body Image: The Risks of Performance-Enhancing Drugs*. Berkeley Heights, NJ: Enslow Publishers, 2005.

Romanowski, Bill. *Romo: My Life on the Edge*. New York, NY: Harper, 2006.

Schaefer, Adam Richard. *Health at Risk: Steroids*. Ann Arbor, MI: Cherry Lake Publishing, 2008.

Walker, Ida. *Steroids: Pumped Up and Dangerous*. Broomall, PA: Mason Crest Publishers, 2007.

BIBLIOGRAPHY

Boniface, Dan. "Broncos Release Punter Todd Sauerbraun." 9NEWS.com, December 18, 2007. Retrieved November 2008 (http://www.9news.com/includes/tools/print.aspx?storyid=83002).

CBSNews.com. "'Romo' Comes Clean: Bill Romanowski Talks to Scott Pelley About Deliberate Violence and Steroid Use." *60 Minutes*, October 16, 2005. Retrieved November 2008 (http://www.cbsnews.com/stories/2005/10/13/60minutes/main941102.shtml).

CBSNews.com. "Steroids Prescribed to NFL Players—Report: 3 Carolina Panthers Filled Prescriptions Before Super Bowl." *60 Minutes*, March 30, 2005. Retrieved November 2008 (http://www.cbsnews.com/stories/2005/03/29/60II/main683747.shtml).

Chaney, Matt. "Dianabol, the First Widely Used Steroid Turns 50 This Year." *New York Daily News*, June 16, 2008. Retrieved November 2008 (http://www.nydailynews.com/sports/football/2008/06/14/2008-06-14_dianabol_the_first_widely_used_steroid_t.html?print=1&page=all).

Egelko, Bob. "Stubblefield Pleads Guilty to Steroid Lies." *San Francisco Chronicle*, January 19, 2008. Retrieved November 2008 (http://sfgate.com/cgi-bin/article.cgi?f=/c/a/2008/01/19/BAJ6UHOOH.DTL).

Eskenazi, Gerald. "Taking a Stance Against Steroids in the NFL." *New York Times*, August 24, 1989. Retrieved November 2008 (http://query.nytimes.com/gst/fullpage.html?res=950DE1DB1E39F937A1575BC0A96F948260).

ESPN.com. "NFL to Test for More Performance-Enhancing Drugs." January 24, 2007. Retrieved November 2008 (http://sports.espn.go.com/nfl/news/story?id=2741136).

ESPN.com. "Report: Panthers Ignored Risk of 'Alarming' Drug Use." August 29, 2006. Retrieved November 2008 (http://sports.espn.go.com/nfl/news/story?id=2563563).

Fainaru-Wada, Mark, and T. J. Quinn. "How U.S. Sports Measure Up to the 'Gold Standard' of Testing." ESPN.com, May 23, 2008. Retrieved November 2008 (http://sports.espn.go.com/espn/columns/story?id=3408547).

Fainaru-Wada, Mark, and T. J. Quinn. "U.S. Pro Sports Teams Still Trail in Drugs-Testing Arms Race." ESPN.com, May 23, 2008. Retrieved November 2008 (http://sports.espn.go.com/espn/columns/story?id=3408399).

Lidz, Franz. "Looking Out for No. 1." *Sports Illustrated*, December 22, 2003. Retrieved November 2008 (http://vault.sportsillustrated.cnn.com/vault/article/magazine/MAG1030900/index.htm).

Murray, Ken. "NFL Now Faces Its Own Steroids Test." *Chicago Tribune*, March 31, 2005. Retrieved November 2008 (http://www.chicagotribune.com/news/local/bal-sp.steroids31mar31,0,624452.story).

New York Times. "Titan Considers Steroids Case Closed." August 14, 2008. Retrieved November 2008 (http://www.nytimes.com/2008/08/14/sports/football/14camps.html).

NIDA. "Facts on Drugs: Anabolic Steroids." NIDA for Teens. Retrieved November 2008 (http://teens.drugabuse.gov/facts/facts_ster1.asp).

Puma, Mike. "Not the Size of the Dog in the Fight." ESPN.com. Retrieved November 2008 (http://espn.go.com/classic/biography/s/Alzado_Lyle.html).

Schmidt, Michael S. "Steroid Dealer Who Cooperated with NFL Is Found Dead." *New York Times*, June 6, 2008. Retrieved November 2008 (http://www.nytimes.com/2008/06/06/sports/football/06jacobs.html?scp=6&sq=NFL%20Steroids%20&st=cse).

Schmidt, Michael S. "Steroid Maker Says He Taught About NFL Loopholes." *New York Times*, May 2, 2008. Retrieved November 2008 (http://www.nytimes.com/2008/05/02/sports/football/02drugs.html?scp=9&sq=NFL%20Steroids%20&st=cse).

Schmidt, Michael S., and Judy Battista. "Drug Tests Could Lead to 8 Suspensions in NFL." *New York Times*, October 24, 2008. Retrieved November 2008 (http://www.nytimes.com/2008/10/25/sports/football/25drugs.html).

Schrotenboer, Brent. "Milestone Moments in the NFL's Performance-Enhancing Drug History." *San Diego Union-Tribune*, September 21, 2008.

Retrieved November 2008 (http://www.signonsandiego.com/sports/nfl/20080921-9999-1s21nfltim.html).

Smith, Timothy W. "NFL's Steroid Policy Too Lax, Doctor Warns." *New York Times*, July 3, 1991. Retrieved November 2008 (http://query.nytimes.com/gst/fullpage.html?res=9D0CEEDB1E3DF930A35754C0A967958260).

Wood, Skip. "Attorney Denies Saints' Lehr Is Target of Steroids Probe." *USA Today*, April 9, 2008. Retrieved November 2008 (http://www.usatoday.com/sports/football/nfl/2008-04-08-steroids-investigation_N.htm).

INDEX

About the Author

After earning a bachelor's degree in English literature at McGill University in Montreal, Canada, author Michael Sommers earned a master's degree in history and civilizations from the École des Hautes Études en Sciences Sociales in Paris, France. For the last fifteen years, Sommers has worked as a writer and photographer. He has previously written other drug-related titles for Rosen, among them *Steroids and Your Muscles* and *Cocaine*.

Photo Credits

Cover, p. 1 (foreground) © Jim McIsaac/Getty Images; cover, pp. 1, 3, 7, 13, 17, 23, 31 (background) © Hisham Ibrahim/Getty Images; pp. 3, 7, 13, 17, 23, 31 (foreground) © Nick Laham/Getty Images; pp. 4, 8 (background), 14, 20, 28, 35 (background) © www.istockphoto.com/Nick M. Do; p. 5 © Greg Trott/Getty Images; pp. 8, 34 © AP Photos; pp. 9, 11 © NFL Photos/Getty Images; p. 15 © Focus on Sport/Getty Images; p. 16 © Getty Images; p. 18 © George Gojkovitch/Getty Images; p. 19 © Ron Sachs/CNP/Corbis; p. 21 © Charles E. Rotkin/Corbis; p. 24 © David Paul Morris/Getty Images; pp. 26, 27 © Al Messerschmidt/NFL Photos/Getty Images; p. 29 © Simon Bruty/Allsport/Getty Images; p. 32 © G. Newman Lawrence/Getty Images; p. 35 © Courtney Perry/Dallas Morning News/Corbis; p. 37 © Tim Umphrey/Corbis.

Designer: Nicole Russo; Editor: Christopher Roberts;
Photo Researcher: Marty Levick